MW00800552

Deluxe Album of
FIDDLE WALTZES
& SLOW AIRS

For One, Two, or Three Violins

by Bill Guest

Online Audio   www.melbay.com/94092BCDEB

Audio Contents

1 2 3 4 5 6 7 8 9 0

Contents

White Orchids

VIOLIN 1

Bill Guest

White Orchids

VIOLIN 2

Bill Guest

White Orchids

VIOLIN 3

Bill Guest

Lilies White And Roses Red

VIOLIN 1

Bill Guest

Lilies   White And Roses Red

VIOLIN 2

Lilies White And Roses Red

VIOLIN 3

Shannon Julianne's Waltz

VIOLIN 1

Bill Guest

Shannon Julianne's Waltz

VIOLIN 2

Shannon Julianne's Waltz

VIOLIN 3

Autumn Fantasies

Bill Guest
Kimberley Isenor

VIOLIN 1

Autumn Fantasies

VIOLIN 2

13

Bill's Rhapsody

VIOLIN 1

Bill Guest

Bill's Rhapsody

VIOLIN 2

Arranged By
Ken Davidson

15

Kaleb's Waltz

VIOLIN 1

Bill Guest
Kimberley Isenor

Kaleb's Waltz

VIOLIN 2

Morning Mist

VIOLIN 1

Bill Guest

Morning Mist

VIOLIN 2

Rebecca's Waltz

VIOLIN 1

Bill Guest

Rebecca's Waltz

VIOLIN 2

"Reflections"

VIOLIN1

Bill Guest
10/2/85

22

"Reflections"

VIOLIN 2

Twilight Hours

VIOLIN 1

Bill Guest
10/5/85

Twilight Hours

VIOLIN 2

The Lonely Gypsy

VIOLIN 1

Bill Guest

The Lonely Gypsy

VIOLIN 2

Londonderry Lament

VIOLIN 1

Bill Guest 1985

Londonderry Lament

VIOLIN 2

Moonlight Over The Rockies

VIOLIN 1

Bill Guest

Moonlight Over The Rockies

VIOLIN 2

31

Aaron's Waltz

VIOLIN 1

Bill Guest

Aaron's Waltz

VIOLIN 2

A Purple Rose

VIOLIN 1

Bill Guest

A Purple Rose

VIOLIN 2

The Blue Eyed Fiddler

VIOLIN 1

Bill Guest

The Blue Eyed Fiddler

VIOLIN 2

Crystal Dawn

VIOLIN 1

Bill Guest

Crystal Dawn

VIOLIN 2

Fantasy Waltz

VIOLIN 1

Bill Guest

Fantasy Waltz

VIOLIN 2

Fireplace Waltz

VIOLIN 1

Bill Guest

Fireplace Waltz

VIOLIN 2

First Time Waltz

VIOLIN 1

Kimberley J. Isenor
Bill Guest

First Time Waltz

VIOLIN 2

Halifax Waltz

VIOLIN 1

Bill Guest

Halifax Waltz

VIOLIN 2

Jacqueline's Waltz

VIOLIN 1

Bill Guest

Jacqueline's Waltz

VIOLIN 2

Jodi's Waltz

VIOLIN1

Bill Guest

Jodi's Waltz

VIOLIN 2

Kelli's Waltz

VIOLIN 1

Bill Guest

Kelli's Waltz

VIOLIN 2

53

Kimberley Jean's Waltz

VIOLIN 1

Bill Guest

Kimberley Jean's Waltz

VIOLIN 2

Kimberley's Theme

VIOLIN 1

Bill Guest

Kimberley's Theme

VIOLIN 2

Linda's Waltz

VIOLIN 1

Bill Guest

Linda's Waltz

VIOLIN 2

Michelle's Waltz

VIOLIN 1

Bill Guest

Michelle's Waltz

VIOLIN 2

Nova Scotia Waltz

VIOLIN 1

Bill Guest

Nova Scotia Waltz

VIOLIN 2

Patti's Waltz

VIOLIN 1

Bill Guest

Patti's Waltz

VIOLIN 2

Peach Blossoms

VIOLIN 1

Bill Guest

Peach Blossoms

VIOLIN 2

Peggy's Cove

VIOLIN 1

Bill Guest

Peggy's Cove

VIOLIN 2

Rosewood Waltz

VIOLIN 1

Bill Guest

Rosewood Waltz

VIOLIN 2

Snowdrift Waltz

VIOLIN 1

Bill Guest

Snowdrift Waltz

VIOLIN 2

Snow On The Mountain

VIOLIN 1

Bill Guest

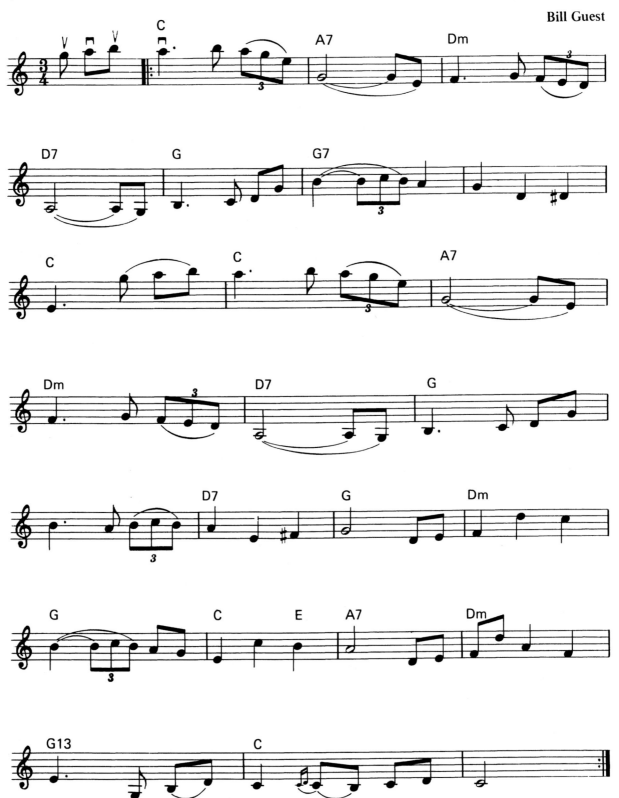

Snow On The Mountain

VIOLIN 2

Soft As A Whisper

VIOLIN 1

Bill Guest

Soft As A Whisper

VIOLIN 2

Bill Guest

The Sparrow's Delight

VIOLIN 1

Bill Guest

The Sparrow's Delight

VIOLIN 2

Suzanne's Waltz

VIOLIN 1

Bill Guest

Suzanne's Waltz

VIOLIN 2

Tiffany's Waltz

VIOLIN 1

Bill Guest

Tiffany's Waltz

VIOLIN 2

Tracey's Waltz

VIOLIN 1

Bill Guest

Tracey's Waltz

VIOLIN 2

Tuxedo Waltz

VIOLIN 1

Bill Guest

Tuxedo Waltz

VIOLIN 2

Apple Blossom Waltz

VIOLIN 1

Bill Guest

Apple Blossom Waltz

VIOLIN 2

Caprice Waltz

VIOLIN 1

Bill Guest

Caprice Waltz

VIOLIN 2

Gretchen's Waltz

VIOLIN 1

Bill Guest

Gretchen's Waltz

VIOLIN 2

Nicole's Waltz

VIOLIN 1

Bill Guest

Nicole's Waltz

VIOLIN 2

Musquodoboit Valley Waltz

VIOLIN 1

Bill Guest

Musquodoboit Valley Waltz

VIOLIN 2

Carol Ann Wheeler's Waltz

VIOLIN 1

Bill Guest 6/85

Carol Ann Wheeler's Waltz

VIOLIN 2

Cole Harbor Waltz

VIOLIN 1

Bill Guest

Cole Harbor Waltz

VIOLIN 2

Sleepytime Waltz

VIOLIN 1

Bill Guest

Sleepytime Waltz

VIOLIN 2

Sunset Over The Islands

VIOLIN 1

Bill Guest

Sunset Over The Islands

VIOLIN 2

Penguine Waltz

Bill Guest

Saturday Night Waltz

Bill Guest

Ontario Waltz

Bill Guest

Soft Wind In The Willows

Bill Guest

Spring Blossoms

Bill Guest

Goldenrod Waltz

Bill Guest

Maple Sugar Waltz

Bill Guest

116

Carl Elliott's Favorite

Bill Guest